SUPRIYA SINGH

WHEN LIFE F*CKS

Guts to Glory

BEEJA HOUSE

BEEJA
HOUSE

ISBN: 978-93-93635-08-2 **(Paperback)**

Published by: Beeja House

First Printing Edition 2022

Contents

DEDICATION

This book is dedicated to all my lovely readers, I hope this book inspires you and builds you up to be stronger and gives you the courage to overcome all battles of your life gracefully.

I dedicate this book to my kids and my Mom, who has been the apple of my everything. They have made me proud again and again. I am blessed to have them and obsessed with them. This book wouldn't have been possible without their constant and well-grounded support always. They have encouraged and uplifted me to achieve every milestone, by fighting the battle called life with me. Without them, my life's journey wouldn't have been the same. I wouldn't be doing all that I do now.

I also dedicate this book to my God, who gave me the power to write the truth.

ACKNOWLEDGEMENT

I would like to thank myself first for rising stronger and emerging as a survivor, not a victim.

I would like to thank God as well as my kids and my mom who believed in me.

I would also like to thank my mentor Geetika Saigal, founder of Beeja Education, who herself is the bestselling author of two amazing books, for guiding me throughout the process.

I am also grateful for every person who has come into my life as a true blessing.

THE DEATH OF INNOCENCE

Once upon a time, it was the onset of winter in the year 1982. There was a middle-class Maharashtrian family who lived in a row house in Mumbai. A lady named Jovita with her two sons named Victor and Albert with their wives Kenny and Rita stayed together as a joint family. Victor was elder and served as a fabric knitting designer machine man in a company in Mumbai. Albert worked as a labourer in the nearby company, whereas Kenny and Rita were housewives. Victor and Kenny's had a love marriage whereas Albert and Rita had an arranged one. Kenny was a beautiful, kind, educated woman with a fair complexion and sharp features while Victor was a tall and handsome guy with a generous heart. Albert and Rita were average looking, though appeared to be nice. Jovita was an old lady who was mostly found cooking while sitting on the floor in the kitchen. Victor and Kenny were soon going to invite a joyous ride to their home as they were expecting their first child.

After a couple of days, early morning, in the nearby hospital, Kenny was admitted due to labour pain. At *4:23 am* Kenny gave birth to a baby girl. The baby was too adorable with blue eyes and a fair complexion. The doctor was amazed by seeing the baby, he declared that Queen Victoria was born in a Maharashtrian family. Victor and Kenny were very happy. She was named Victoria. After 3 days, they returned home from the hospital. Everyone was happy at home, a newborn was welcomed by the family. Kenny was busy taking care of her little one, Jovita also had 4 daughters, who were elder to Victor. Two of them were married to Jovita's younger brothers, who often visited their home. One of them named Laura with her husband Patrick visited home from Indonesia and had got too many dresses and toys for little Victoria. As Laura and Patrick had been staying out of India for quite a long time, they often consumed alcohol. All the family members had a party including Victor and Jovita joined Laura for a couple of drinks. As long as Laura stayed in their home, Victor started taking alcohol every day. Soon after, Laura and Patrick returned back to their home in Amritsar as they were transferred to India now. Victor started drinking alcohol on daily basis at home. Jovita never stopped him, as a mother, in fact, she also joined him for drinks sometimes. Victoria was growing day by day. Kenny was upset with Victor's drinking habit, she requested "Victor, please don't drink daily." Victor promised he won't drink, but every evening while coming back home from his work, he started halting at liquor bars and came home fully out of his control, completely drunk, as he was now addicted to alcohol.

In spite of several requests and warnings from Kenny, Victor couldn't stop drinking. When Victoria turned 3 years old, arguments started between Victor and Kenny and little Victoria was the spectator of these fights. Victor was completely driven to alcohol and distracted from his work and arguments continued to increase between the two. As a result, Kenny went back to her maiden house with Victoria. Kenny's parents looked after Victoria and Kenny, Kenny completed her last year of graduation. But Victoria's Dad, Victor was so alcoholic and short-tempered that every day he visited Victoria and created a chaos at Kenny's house. Kenny was ashamed to see her parents getting embarrassed in front of society, so she decided to return back home with Victor.

As Victor neglected his work, due to his drinking habits, he lost his job. Victor's sister Laura who lived in Amritsar offered him a job in her husband's company, as a result, Victor and Kenny moved to Amritsar with little Victoria.

Laura and Patrick never had their own child, due to some medical complications which is why Laura loved to stay with little Victoria and considered her as her own daughter. Often, she asked Victor and Kenny to adopt Victoria legally, but Victor and Kenny never agreed to it, Staying together Laura had developed an attachment towards Victoria, Victoria had turned 4 years old and started going to playschool, where she found new friends who spoke the Punjabi language. She met new people and a new environment apart from home, learning a new language. She was always excited to go to her playschool. The outside world started changing for her but the inside world of her parents was the same, the arguments and the fights continued. The chaos never left her mind.

Victor's alcohol addiction was up to the next level, he again started neglecting his new job and often stayed home drinking throughout the day, when Kenny stopped him from doing so, he started abusing her verbally and soon domestic violence started. Victoria's mom Kenny was badly beaten by her dad, Victor. After watching such abuse at home, Victoria was terrified, she used to hide to avoid violence. A poor child couldn't find out what was wrong in her home.

A few months later, Victor again lost his job due to his alcohol addiction. Laura being an elder sister never stopped Victor from drinking. Patrick had good friends in Delhi. He requested one of his friends for a new job for Victor in Delhi, looking his skills in Machines, he was offered a job in Delhi, as a result now again this family shifted to Delhi. It was a new place for Victoria, her friends were left behind and her new school and new friends made her try to adapt to the new surroundings. A few months later, in spite of taking contraceptive pills, Kenny had conceived, Victoria was happy as she was becoming a sister soon to some little newborn baby.

Kenny gave birth to another cute little baby girl, Victoria's sister was born, and they welcomed a new family member, she was named Princess. Victor and Kenny were busy taking care of newborns. Victoria loved touching small babies, she was always excited to hold them, but Mom didn't allow it as Victoria was too small to carry the baby. Victoria started feeling ignored as both her parents were more loving and caring for Princess. She felt neglected like every first child feels when the second child is born but Victoria was very happy as she noticed the world for her was changing as her Dad had started improving slowly, Victoria enjoyed the company of her little sister Princess. Victoria prayed to God, "Please, please God! Let my father and mother never fight again, please keep us all happy."

Victoria often watched other children happy around her with their parents. She always dreamt of a happy family like others. Day by day passed by with her prayers to God, every evening she had the fear that now Victor will be drunk and a fight might start, she was in a state of confusion, disorder, uncertainty and great anxiety, always with fear of a fight by Victor. Time went on smoothly for a few months but this peace couldn't last for too long, soon the fights and arguments and physical abuse started with Kenny, and Victoria was the witness to all. Princess was a baby unaware of the situation at home. Due to Victor's drinking habit, he once again lost his job.

Victor requested his sister Laura for a new job and asked for a reference from Patrick. Patrick asked his friend and Victor was offered a new job in Gujarat Vadodara, as a result again the entire family was shifted to Gujarat. Now, Victoria was in grade 2 and her sister Princess started going to playschool. Once again Victoria's friends were left behind, again new friends, a new school, new people who spoke the Gujarati language. A completely new environment. Victoria always kept praying to God "Please, please God! This time there should be no fights between my parents, I want a happy family."

For one year everything went on smoothly in Victoria's family. Then again, fights and domestic violence started now that Victoria reached grade 3. Victor's addiction increased, he started neglecting his work and again he lost his job. Yet again, Victor asked for Patrick and Laura's help. With Patrick's reference, he got a new job opportunity in Mumbai itself. He needed to join the new job immediately, so he went to Mumbai and started staying with his mother Jovita and Brother Albert and his wife Rita. Kenny stayed back in Gujarat with Victoria and Princess as it was in the middle of the session of grade 3 for Victoria, but in a few days, Victor came back to Vadodara and said, "I am not feeling well for the last few days, Albert's wife doesn't cook for me. Mother is not keeping well either. Kenny please come with me to Mumbai and drop this academic year for Victoria." When Victoria learnt this news, she did not agree to leave the school in between the session and waste her one year, she convinced her parents that she can't leave her studies like this. Victor and Kenny decided to ask for help from their house owners, where they lived on rent, which was a bungalow, where the first floor was rented by Victor's family, they requested the owners of the house to take care of Victoria's food, as they were leaving for Mumbai due to some problems and would not want to waste her academic year, she decided to stay back and complete her year with the help of owner's family, she was 9 years old. Victor, Kenny and Princess moved to Mumbai.

The owner's family had 2 children, one boy and one girl. It was a typical Gujarati family. Victoria stayed with the family as a paying guest for 5 months. She was happy that now she was not a part of domestic violence and an abusive atmosphere. They were unknown people, but she adjusted to them. As she stayed as a paying guest in that house, the owner's lady instructed, " Victoria, you will have to wash your own clothes, do your dishes, clean your room and organise your belongings properly, it's your responsibility now, I will give only food to you." Victoria nodded her head and agreed to follow her instructions. Within a few days, she had very well learnt to organize her things, do all her work on her own, wash clothes and utensils, clean her room, study and manage toiletries. Only food was given by the owner's lady. Everything was good but the owner's lady hated giving her a full meal, whenever her own children asked for more rice or bread she would happily give more, but when Victoria asked, she replied, "Food is over now, drink water and go to sleep," but Victoria never complained about this to anyone as she was afraid she would have to leave the school in between. She always slept with an empty stomach just because she couldn't leave school in mid-session. She decided to stay till the completion of the course. Soon exams were over and the academic year ended.

Victoria came to Mumbai after spending 5 months with unknown people. She was happy to see her sister Princess as she had started going to school now. Here, they lived in a joint family which consisted of Victor's mother and Brother Albert, who also had 2 daughters now. Again, it was a different world for Victoria staying with unknown people. Victoria and her sister Princess were very good at studies, they came first in school. It was again a new school and new friends for Victoria, the world was constantly changing for her. Victor's addiction to alcohol had increased and domestic violence had started, this time along with Victoria's mom Kenny, Victoria was also beaten and bruised by Victor. Victoria was unable to make out why her dad was beating her without reason, she was terrified even talking to her dad, going to school only saved her. Despite all the suffering and physical abuse, she never left the sight of her academics. She performed well in her studies, Kenny started teaching in school as well as taking home tuition. Victor would hardly go to work, he would rather stay at home drinking all day, abusing or sleeping. For everyone else, the home was the place of only chaos and abuse. Victor stayed home most of the time. He would never have money for alcohol too, he'd ask for it from Kenny but whenever she'll refuse to give it to him, Victor wouldn't listen to her and forcefully take it from her to buy alcohol. Whenever Kenny refused to give him money, he used to abuse her badly. None of the family members came to rescue Kenny from Victor's physical assault. All were simply spectators, watching them fight and verbally saying, "Please Victor, don't hit Kenny" very loudly. Princess was too young, she used to hide behind Victoria, unaware of what was happening with her parents and when Victoria went for her mom's help, she was even beaten badly by her dad.

Victoria always wondered why Jovita, Albert and Rita never came for help to save them. She spoke to her Granny Jovita, "Grandma, why doesn't Albert beat Rita like how my dad hit my mom?" She said, "You don't worry dear, everything will be good one day." Victoria was growing day by day, she was 11 years old. She started thinking about this problem of her parents, as her mind was working on a solution continuously. Not only did her mind start thinking but her body was also growing into a beautiful woman. At the very first stage, her breast became visible, like all other girls' bodies going through an initial physical appearance change. The man around her, Uncle Albert always noticed her, when she sat on the bench of their home backyards, where there was a guava tree, beside the toilets. He often got her chocolates whenever he used to return from Dubai and visited home every year. He spoke to Victoria very often, as he spoke to his two daughters. One evening, there was huge fight between Victor and Kenny, and Victoria was also badly beaten, somehow uncle Albert came in for help and stopped the fight, and took Victor out of the house. Victoria thought she should ask for her Uncle's help to stop her father's alcohol addiction. One afternoon, Victoria was sitting under the guava tree in the backyard of her house beside the toilet.

Albert saw her and sat beside her. He said, "Hey dear, why are you sitting here?" Victoria said, "Everybody is sleeping in the house, even Mom is not at home, all my friends would come to play in the evening." Victoria asked, "Why can't you stop my father from drinking? As he is your brother, dad would listen to you."

Albert replied, "I will definitely tell Victor not to drink, you don't worry my child," and kept his hands on her shoulders, slowly started moving the palm and fingers around her breast, touching her breast slowly saying, "Thik hai babu! I will ask your dad not to drink". Victoria was 11 years old, she could hardly understand what was happening but she couldn't make out why her uncle was touching her body so weirdly. She removed her uncle's hand from her shoulders and moved aside. It was difficult for her to understand this activity of her Uncle.

Albert had come for a holiday of one month. As he served in Dubai for one year, whenever Albert saw Victoria alone, he purposely came to talk to her and somehow managed to touch her breast and other body parts weirdly. Victoria started to avoid talking to Uncle Albert and escaped whenever Uncle approached her to talk.

Victoria's dad had left the job and was staying at home drinking from morning till night. The alcohol shop was near the house, hardly a few minutes' distance away in the slum area. He started sending Victoria to the liquor shop to purchase alcohol for him. Victoria hated it, but if she refused to go, he would beat her. It was a tough time for Victoria as she was ashamed of going to such an area as people from school might notice her, she was embarrassed to face her friends.

One afternoon, when everyone in the house had gone for some wedding function, one of the neighbourhood's uncles who was Victoria's uncle Albert's friend visited her home. This time Victoria was alone at home studying, he came near her and asked for water. Victoria went into the kitchen to get water for him, but as she left, he followed her into the kitchen and started weirdly touching Victoria. He opened his pants zip and removed his penis and asked her to hold it.

Victoria started crying, refusing to do so, but he pulled her towards him and closed her mouth with one hand and forcefully gave it her hands while touching her breast with the other hand and suddenly something was released from that penis. Victoria was crying and asking him to leave her, now he removed a handkerchief from his pocket and wiped the thing which was on the floor and ran out of the house, Victoria was petrified by this incident.

Victoria was in tears when all the family members were back home. She told her father and mother about this incident. Her dad was totally out of alcohol as he could not even stand on his feet, he collapsed into bed. Her mom was angry to hear this, she wanted to go and hit that man, but couldn't gather the strength to do so. She told Victoria, "My child, I am so sorry for leaving you alone at home, please stop crying." Kenny tried to console her by saying, "I promise I would never leave you alone at home from now onwards, I will always be with you." Victoria stopped crying and started to argue with Kenny, "Why did you marry my father? Why all of them are so bad here? why did you give birth to me?"

Kenny was listening quietly to Victoria as she knew she had given a very bad life to Victoria.

She tried to calm her down saying "I am sorry, for putting you in such a situation, please calm down." Victoria went to sleep after crying for some time. Victoria decided to focus on her studies. She wanted to become something and achieve success through her studies so that she could be out of this environment, but the atmosphere at home was pathetic and awful. She wondered why on earth she was born. Her dad's addiction and violence were at their peak, in order to escape Victor's beatings, her mom ran out of the house as her dad started beating her but Victoria refused to run as she was afraid of neighbours and people around would tease her, no one came to resolve fights, but everyone was ready to laugh at her.

Despite all the chaos, she concentrated on her studies. Victoria was 14 years old and now growing into a beautiful girl. She started getting love proposals in the form of letters from her schoolmates and tuition buddies, like all teenagers she too liked that attention given to her. Now Victoria was in grade 9, where studies were the most important part of her life.

Verbal and physical abuse continued and had worsened. All her body was swollen and bruised most of the time. It was difficult for her to sit on the school bench. She had made up her mind to get out of this house and chaos. Now she decided to run away from her house.

THE DEVASTATION

Victoria decided that they would run away and stay separate from her father but couldn't convince her mother. Life continued for Victoria as she was helpless and couldn't stop suffering and no one came to help her family. Princess too was growing up, in these awful circumstances. It was very humiliating for these young girls to face the people in the neighbourhood as well as school. Victor's addiction increased and his health started deteriorating but his behaviour was the same, as violent and abusive towards his family. One day, in a nearby bank, Kenny met one of her neighbours Garry, who was an old lady and the mother of a 32-year-old man. She knew about Kenny's problems and Victor's alcohol addiction, she casually suggested, "I know a *pandit* who can help in solving Victor's alcohol addiction," Kenny was glad to hear that, where she also said, "Whenever Victor starts beating you, run away from there and come to my house for some time, to escape his beatings." Kenny was thankful to the lady and they departed. Victor started demanding money from Kenny as usual and as she denied it, he started beating Kenny, now she ran away out of the house with Princess to Garry's home in the neighbourhood. Victoria hesitated to run away like this but after taking a few beatings, when

Victor threw a big iron rod toward Victoria, she also ran behind Kenny to the widow lady's house. All three stayed there for 2 hours waiting for Victor to sleep or go out of the house.

Garry was a kind hearted lady, who tried to help Kenny and her daughters. She gave some food to them and said, "You three have to fight this battle together, escaping from Victor's abuse." Garry's son Peter came into the house, who was 32 years old and spoke politely to all of them. Victoria found those people to be good. She was happy that at least there was one family who was ready to support her to escape the hard times. Gradually Victoria, Princess and Kenny spent most of their time escaping from Victor's abuse in this family's house. Garry also took Kenny to that *pandit* to solve Victor's addiction. That lady's son Peter appeared to be very friendly to these three. Victoria had found a big brother in his soul and she was happy that she found that care and friendship both in one person who she thought was her big brother, he became like a fatherly figure for Victoria. Peter took Victoria shopping and made her feel special as she grew to be 15 years old. Peter started using Victoria's faith for him as a weapon to come close to her. He tried to convince Victoria that she should start earning and help her family as her dad was jobless and completely out of money and the family was suffering a financial crisis.

Instead of concentrating on her studies, Victoria started thinking about how she could come out of this situation and start earning along with her studies. Domestic violence had increased and there was no way to stop this. One day early morning, Victoria, Princess and her mother finally escaped from that house before her dad could make out, with no luggage, no clothes and no money. All three escaped finally from that house and visited Kenny's friend and asked her to arrange for a rental flat for them. Victoria's mother hardly had any money, she sold whatever jewellery she had and was able to rent a flat. On the first day, staying at a rented flat with Princess and mom without their dad, they felt like heaven, although they slept on the bare floor using Kenny's saree as blankets, but the peace of mind they had was priceless.

Victoria and Princess started going to school from their new rented house but the locality there was not good. They started gossiping about Victoria's mother as a single lady staying with two young daughters. Victoria was followed by roadside Romeos to school and back. A different kind of suffering started for Victoria now. Boys followed her teasing her whenever she stepped out of the house, she found it embarrassing and difficult to deal with this situation, so she convinced her mother to shift to another area to rent a flat and as a result, the family shifted to another society.

Society accepted women to stay with addicted husbands and bare all sufferings and abuse, but couldn't accept single women living alone with two young daughters. Women staying with no man in the house was a curse for single women. People looked at them from a very different angle. They were least respected and projected characterless women who would stay alone without their man of the house. Other women around her also looked at her differently. Kenny was beautiful in her looks and women envied her for it. People around passed demeaning comments whenever she passed by the society. Victor was worried as he couldn't find out where his family disappeared all of a sudden, but instead of searching for them, he was drowned in his drinks. One day, he realized that he could find Victoria in her school, so he visited her school completely drunk and created a scene in front of the school. Victoria's school Principal called Victoria to meet her father in the middle of the class. Victoria was annoyed to see her dad in school, he tried to convince Victoria to come back home, but she refused and asked him to go back home. Now Victoria's dad made it a daily ritual to visit Victoria's school completely drunk. One day, at 11 am, he came to school and asked to meet Victoria at the gate of the school, but when watchman refused to let him in, He started shouting and abusing the school and teachers, saying, "I would kill everyone in school, send Victoria to meet me immediately." The school's Principal was fed up with this act, she warned Victoria that this can't be continued any longer.

Victoria slowly started losing interest in her studies, there seemed no solution to her problem. She was trying to figure out how this suffering would end. Victoria's dad now started visiting her mom's workplace drunk and creating scenes, even her mom lost her job due to problems created by her drunken husband. Now her mom was also jobless. After a few days, the widowed lady Garry and her son Peter visited Victoria's home. He fixed a job for Kenny in a jewellery shop. It was a standing job of 12 hours. She started working in a jewellery shop, and both the girls again started to concentrate on their studies. Peter visited Victoria's house very often, her mother left home at 8 am in the morning and would return back home directly at 8 pm in the evening. Victoria had morning school and her sister Princess had afternoon school. He used to visit Victoria's house when she was alone at home.

Victoria believed that he was a very kind and helpful man, who was interested in helping their family, she thought she was blessed to have a brother like him. He somehow convinced Victoria to get a job and told her he would help her to achieve her dreams and be financially independent. One day, he told Victoria that he had fixed some part-time job for her. He took Victoria with him to a hotel and said the person who has the job would come within a while and he gave her a glass of juice, mixed with some kind of tablet in it. She was unconscious after drinking the juice.

This man Peter who was like a trusted brother to victoria turned out to be evil and raped her badly, Victoria was unaware of the activity that happened to her, she was into a deep sleep. Victoria's mother was in search of her but couldn't find her, so she launched a police complaint about missing Victoria, at the nearest police station. Police immediately took action and helped her find Victoria. After some time, the police found out that Victoria was in a hotel, when the police and Kenny reached the hotel and knocked the door, Peter opened the door and tried to run away as he saw police in front. Victoria was still asleep, after some sprinkles of water on her face, Victoria came to consciousness. She started crying after seeing her mother Kenny and got up from bed asking, "what happened Mom and why my stomach is paining so much," she couldn't make out that she was raped by Peter. Police arrested Peter and took him to the police station. Victoria returned home with her mother, Kenny asked her to take bath and clean herself thoroughly and explained to her, "Peter has raped you poor child when you were unconscious, so you didn't realise it, but this is the reason for your severe stomach pain." Victoria now came to know that this man Peter has forcefully inserted his Penis into Victoria's Vagina, so her mom is saying that she is raped, she was frightened by the incident that happened to her. Sister Princess couldn't make out what was wrong with Victoria, the poor child was terrified seeing Victoria weeping throughout.

This year was a crucial year for Victoria as she was in grade 10 and board exams were on the way but Victoria mostly missed school and stayed at home weeping and suffering 'why she was the one to suffer since childhood?' Despite being good in her studies, due to lack of attendance and nuisance created in school by Victoria's dad, the Principal did not allow her to appear for her board exams. This took Victoria into acute depression. On the other side, her dad Victor and his brother Albert decided to sell the house as Victor demanded his share in the property because he wanted money to buy alcohol, so Mother Jovita and two brothers sold their house and all the family members got their own share of the money. Albert and his wife and mother Jovita bought a new house in the nearby location. Victor was left alone with money but no house. He stayed in that house till the new owners took possession. Victor was destroying all the money he got into alcohol. After a few days, new owners of the house came to stay in, so Victor had to leave home. Victor stayed in bar for a week, drinking all day and night. Many friends of Victor borrowed money from him, some of them robbed him too, as he was so drunk, he couldn't even realise where his money was disappearing day by day. He stayed outside the bar and slept on the bench at night. A few days passed by and all money he had was already spent by him. He started living with one of his beggar friends who lived across the street in a small hut. Victor now started drinking alcohol on credit, requested the bar manager to give him some alcohol and promise to pay later. Victor was left alone with severe health loss, he would hardly find something to eat. As a result, his physical condition started deteriorating, 80 kg Victor was 40 kg now, his health was falling day by day. One day, early morning, when Kenny was going to the market to fetch some vegetables, one known man informed her, "Kenny, I think your husband Victor has died or is unconscious on the street, I tried to wake him up but he didn't respond." Kenny rushed to see Victor and found him lying on the street with torn and dirty clothes, almost like a poor beggar. She woke him up and as Victor saw Kenny, he started apologising her holding her feet. Seeing Victor in this condition, Kenny couldn't resist herself from helping him, so she brought him home to stay with them.

Victoria and Princess were horrified to see their dad's condition, they felt pity for him, as he looked too unwell. The family had reunited again and started living together in their rented house.

Victor's health issues increased and after several tests, he was diagnosed with severe heart issues, it was discovered that two valves aortic and mitral valve of the heart had failed and the doctor recommended transplant surgery for him to survive longer. His health started deteriorating day by day. Mom could hardly go to work as she was taking care of her bedridden husband. Victoria couldn't appear for her board exams. She was broken and depressed. In that new neighbourhood, she met a girl named Jinny who was a divorced woman with a little daughter, who lived with her mother, father, sister and brother. She worked in a beauty salon. Victoria slowly became friends with her. She frequently visited Victoria's house. She found out very soon what all happened to Victoria since childhood and how she was abused, molested and raped at a very young age.

VICTORIA'S SECRET

Victoria's father's health was worsened so he was admitted to the hospital. The doctor said he can't live without a heart valve transplant. Even Victoria's mom started falling ill, Developed a disease called fissure and fistula. Victoria was 16 years old and her sister Princess was 11 years old and both the girls were helpless. Victoria started working in a salon as a helper to her friend Jinny but couldn't earn enough money. Jinny opened up about her personal life to Victoria. She said, "I had a love marriage with one south Indian guy 6 years ago, but he use to abuse me physically after drinks, so I got divorced from him and now staying alone with my daughter." Victoria was instantly connected to her, after listening to her story of physical abuse and related it to her mother's abuse faced by her father. Victoria was able to understand her situation, day by day Jinny and Victoria became good friends, and both shared with each other, all the past and current situations they were facing. They often had free time at salon, where they had their lunch together every day, within few days they became best friends. Victoria started trusting Jinny, then one day after 2 months, Jinny took Victoria along with her to one party. It was a fun place, a huge club with people dancing, drinking and enjoying having fun. Victoria was fascinated to see such a place for the first time. Jinny introduced her to many people in the club, she enjoyed her time at such a place where there was loud music and happy people around her. She could forget about everything in her life but it was short term fun. Soon the time came when her friend Jinny gave her a soft drink and Victoria started feeling tipsy, soon Victoria realized that Jinny had sold Victoria.

Victoria was drugged and raped, when Victoria got aware of this, she lost faith in everyone around her. Victoria stopped talking to Jinny. Her family ran out of money. Dad was admitted to I.C.U. and her mom was undergoing treatments for fissure and fistula. Victoria decided to talk to Jinny for help, Jinny not only helped her financially but assured Victoria that she can be independent and get her dad operated on soon and get back to normal life, only if she listens to her and visits her clients and sleeps with them as she says. Victoria was completely broken and in need of money, but she had no other choice, by working at any other place she wouldn't have got that amount of money which she needed as she was only 17 years old. She already had been through the worst circumstances and there was no option for her, better than agreeing to Jinny's proposal. Jinny introduced her to a man who was middle-aged. Victoria was helpless about what could happen to her next. She was shattered and devastated as there was no hope left for her.

She was seventeen years old and the aged man whom she met seemed to be a kind man, she prayed to God every time she met that man, but instead of touching her body, that man-made Victoria feed him food sitting in a room. Victoria was comfortable with feeding that man, he was soft-spoken and polite. He said he will be helping her out financially. Victoria told him all the life and situations that had happened to her since childhood. So he first decided to shift Victoria to the new society and helped her by paying bills for the hospital. Victoria's dad's blood pressure wasn't in control to get operated as well as the number of operations was too high. Princess was now completely engaged in her studies. Her dad's blood pressure was now normalized, and he was sent back home for a few days before the operation.

This man who came into Victoria's life tried to help her and asked her to enroll herself on a computer course, as Victoria had not passed her 10th board examination. Now she had some hope to learn something new again. She started going to computer classes. Now, she was hoping to get a better life, something very wrong happened again, that man died due to a heart attack. Victoria lost his support and she was helpless again and left with nothing but the responsibility for her dad's operation and mom's illness. Victoria decided to meet her friend Jinny. So she could help her in this situation. When Victoria met her, she introduced her to one of her girlfriends Paula who used to work for rich people, Paula said to Victoria "I will give you the full 20 lakhs," which she needed for the operation. But only if Victoria agrees to go and meet her clients wherever and whenever asked.

Victoria agreed to Paula's proposal. Time passed by, Victoria's dad was serious due to liver issues and was admitted to the hospital. As per agreement with Paula, Victoria was sent to Delhi to meet some minister, Victoria travelled by flight for the first time and visited this minister. He was her grandfather's age, around 65 years old and Victoria was only 18 years old. This minister asked Victoria to remove her clothes, Victoria found it a little weird but she obeyed him and was standing naked in front of that minister. He came close to her and as he touched her boobs and was released, he was unable to perform any further sexual activity, so this minister asked Victoria to stay back for the night. She agreed to stay back, after some time the minister came back and had dinner with Victoria and again the same thing was repeated this time he asked Victoria to remove her clothes and hold his penis and soon he was released without performing any further intercourse activity. Victoria was sent back to Mumbai the next day. Victoria was paid 3 lac rupees at that very time.

Victoria's dad was taken under supervision in the hospital to resolve liver issues in order to perform the operation. Victoria had to gather 17 lac more for his operation. In her heart, Victoria was wishing her dad to die, but her mom was weeping and convincing her dad to stay strong and he will be alright and soon their family could live a better life now together. Victoria didn't stop as she was on a mission to raise 17 lac rupees more as soon as possible to get her dad back home for good times now. This time Victoria was sent to Darjeeling by Paula where she a met very well-known businessman and industrialist from West Bengal. He was an aged man around 70 years and he specially called Victoria for his son, as his son was in depression and going through an emotional breakdown. When Victoria met this businessman's son, she was shocked to see his behaviour, he was drinking alcohol continuously and consuming cocaine and cigarettes. Victoria was scared of what this man would do to her, but she was sitting quietly next to him. He made Victoria have some alcohol. She was a little tipsy. After some time this man broke down into tears talking about his life story of divorce and misunderstanding with his wife, Victoria also started crying listening to his story. He did not touch Victoria at all, after chatting for a long time, they slept at 3 am at night, but at 6 am early in the morning, that man's father the businessman entered the room. Victoria was terrified to see this man in her room so early. He woke her up and took her to another room next door. There he started removing her clothes and tried to have sexual intercourse with her but he was released at that very moment of touching her body when he touched his penis to her vagina. Then, he asked Victoria to dress up and leave. Victoria returned back home now with 6 lac rupees.

Victoria and her family now were again shifted to a new society on rent. Dad was getting ready for the operation but his blood pressure levels never came down. This time Victoria asked Paula if she had 9 lac rupees and could she help her to get 11 lac more. Paula said she would but it will take some time. In this new society, Victoria met a boy who was 2 years elder than her, his name was Cavin. He was a funny guy. His aunt stayed in the same building as Victoria's house, he often visited his aunt and played with all the society children. Victoria started playing badminton with him and started laughing again. As she had not smiled for a long time, she started laughing due to this guy Cavin. Slowly this boy started falling in love with Victoria. Victoria also liked Cavin, they spent more time together and came close to each other day by day. All the children in the building formed a nice group with Cavin in it. The New Year was coming closer and all of them decided to go to Marine Drive late at night to celebrate New Year's Eve. Cavin and Victoria and two other friends were in one car and the other four friends in another car. Cavin was sitting next to Victoria, trying to crack jokes to seek Victoria's attention. Victoria noticed that Cavin had fallen for her. Victoria too enjoyed his joyful company. They roamed the entire night on Marine Drive holding each other's hand. It was a pleasant feeling for Victoria. As the clock struck

12 midnight Cavin kissed her, and even Victoria kissed him in return. It was a wonderful experience for Victoria, Cavin proposed to Victoria be his girlfriend, Victoria said "yes". After spending some time sitting close to each other on the shores of Marine Drive, they returned back home. After a few days, Cavin's group of friends decided to go on a trip to Shirdi to Sai Baba's temple. Cavin asked Victoria, "My friends and me have planned one small trip to the temple, will you accompany me on this trip?" Victoria said, "Yes, I will come for the trip." The trip day arrived and all of Cavin's friend were in couple, total 4 couples were in the trip. They had hired an XUV car for the trip, playing *antakshari* throughout the road trip they reached Shirdi, they had booked rooms in a cottage, near the temple. Victoria and Cavin shared one room, after having dinner all the friends proceeded to their respective cottage. Victoria and Cavin started talking to each other, lying on the bed. Cavin said "I love you Victoria and I want to marry you." Victoria just kept mum listening to him. Cavin then kissed Victoria, they hugged and the hormones turned high. Both went far into this relationship, they crossed their limits and got sexually intimate and made love, this time it was not forceful for Victoria but out of her own will.

She discovered a new side of her, she was growing into a lover. Cavin pleased Victoria's family with his gentle behaviour and had become good support and friend to the entire family. He wanted to marry Victoria. But Victoria knew it wasn't possible unless she was independent, after all, she had the responsibility of the entire family on her little shoulders.

This time, Victoria was sent to Gujarat by Paula to visit some fabric king. This man was very ugly and dark in complexion, at first sight, Victoria was scared to look at him. This man jumped and kissed Victoria so badly, bruising all over her body, it was painful for Victoria to survive this moment, somehow she managed this sexual activity and returned back home this time with 4 lac rupees. Victoria was terrified of making money like this. It was a very painful and risky job, as well as mental harassment she went through was pathetic. She decided to start some business with that money and make it double. But there was no proper support, she purchased a scooty for her sister Princess so she could learn and travel on her own for her studies. Princess was unaware of whatever was happening in Victoria's life. She concentrated on her studies, Princess was a brilliant student.

Victoria was emotionally involved with Cavin, they decided that they would get married and solve the problem together. Cavin was jobless at that time. Victoria always wondered how she could marry Cavin as he was without a job. Time passed by, Victoria's scooty was not working well, so she asked Cavin to get it repaired from the garage nearby, Cavin took the scooty to the garage. After a few days, things started missing from Victoria's house, like a watch and cream, etc. but she thought it might be somewhere in the house. One fine day, Cavin's sister called Victoria to visit their house. Victoria visited Cavin's house in his absence, Cavin's sister showed her watches and things that Cavin robbed from Victoria's house.

She was shocked to know this. She called Cavin and asked to meet him. He said, "I am with one of my friends in my college," Victoria immediately reached his college, where she found out Cavin was sitting with his ex-girlfriend, when Victoria asked, "Why are you sitting with your ex?" He didn't reply anything but the girl who was sitting with him replied, "I am not his ex, he proposed to me a few days back." This was the second shock for Victoria in one day. She slapped Cavin in front of everyone and when asked about scooty which she gave for repair, that time Cavin disclosed that he had sold the scooty's part to different people and made money for his needs. This situation was so awful and shameful for Victoria to be in love with a guy who betrayed her differently. Victoria was heartbroken completely.

She was 19 years old now. At this age, she was unable to judge people and fall prey to them. She decided not to trust anyone further. After a few days, she was sent to Kolkata by Paula, where she met two brothers from the raw material industry. They appeared good in looks as well as behaviour. They spoke politely to her and roamed around explored new places in Kolkata for two days. They just helped Victoria to get comfortable with them, one of them told Victoria, "You stay here with the elder brother for today and tomorrow I will take you to Bangalore." Victoria agreed. This man was polite and humble. He slept with Victoria and had sex with her in a very decent way without harming her.

Victoria left with the other man for Bangalore the next day. They stayed in a hotel, where he called another man and got intimate with a man in front of Victoria. She was shocked to witness this sexual activity between two men. It was the first time she saw something very unusual. But as far as it was harmless, she was comfortable with it, after all, it was their choice, she was no one to question or judge. After some time, he gave Victoria 4 lac rupees and left and asked Victoria to leave from there, but she couldn't get any flight for Mumbai at that time. So, Victoria had to travel by bus for the first time from Bangalore to Mumbai.

Supriya Singh

THE TWIST OF FATE

Victoria started her bus journey, she was sitting on a bus listening to music and thinking about what kind of life she has got since childhood facing different challenges at different stages and the pain and suffering continued to be the same, talking to herself. "Why does God had chosen me to live in such a pathetic and helpless situation, why me, why me?" She kept talking to God in her mind because she knew she loved too much, she helped too much and never really thought about herself even for once, although no one forced her to take responsibility for the entire family on her shoulders. Then, there wasn't any helping hand from either family members or friends. She had to suffer alone, as there was no other option and she wanted her sister Princess to at least achieve her dreams by studying well and gaining that success and respect from the world. Victoria was assured that Princess would work hard towards her studies and gain success and power. Victoria was no longer a sister now, she had become a mother to her sister. Thinking about all her suffering, she was gazing out of the window of a bus. After a long time, she was alone, sitting for quite a long time thinking and thinking and couldn't stop blaming God for the journey she went through so far now. She said to God, "Are you really there, do you even exist, prove your presence to me, I haven't seen you, why does everyone pray to you, you don't even bother to listen to me, I hate you."

Victoria started listening to songs, trying to forget everything so she could calm herself down, she saw a boy sitting next to the right-side seat of the bus and staring at her. She found it a little weird, she was praying to God "no more suffering please…" after some time that guy kept a cap on his face and went off to sleep. The bus stopped at one restaurant, Victoria got down to have some food and she saw the guy smoking and looking at her. He was a good-looking guy with a good physique, after 30 minutes the bus left that place. Victoria again started listening to music. After a few minutes, that guy asked Victoria, "Where are you from?" She replied, "I am from Mumbai" and the conversation began between the two strangers.

They started speaking to each other in English and eventually dropped to Hindi as the guy Robert said, "I am uncomfortable in communicating in English." Victoria liked the authenticity of that guy, admitting he was poor at speaking and the conversation went on through. His name was Robert, who claimed himself to be a practising boxer, who came to meet his younger brother in Bangalore. The chats between the two went on throughout the night and by morning Victoria had fallen asleep on his shoulder. As she woke up, Robert kissed Victoria on her cheeks. Victoria felt it was a dream, leaning on his shoulder, having that comfortable arm around her neck and she found that this is the place to feel so secure, but soon realized it was happening, hugging in a manner feels the most beautiful form of communication that allows the other person to know beyond that they matter. There was an energetic exchange between the two divine souls which made her realise falling for him wasn't falling at all. It was like she walked into the house and suddenly knew it was home. Victoria knew there is no greater agony than bearing an untold story inside her, but she couldn't disclose it to him. She was thinking about the difference between the sound of her intuition and her trauma misleading her. Something attracted between the two within one night both had fallen for each other, their bodies and souls were interacting with each other in the most pleasant way. She did not want to be away from his arm of comfort and security. Conversation again began about likes, dislikes, and favourites. Robert asked her, "Will you get off of the bus with me in Pune, we will spend some time together, then I will drop you on Mumbai's other bus." Instead of going to Mumbai, Victoria got off of the bus with this guy Robert. Feeling in her mind, "Strength is what you get after facing the madness."

Both couldn't hold their urge to discover each other more. They booked a room in a hotel for one day and got into the room, where they couldn't resist themselves hugging, kissing and unclothing each other. Testosterone and estrogen hormones were at a high level now, they crossed all the limits and got physically intimidated with each other while the overall sex turned out to be magical for them. After spending some more time chit-chatting with each other, and exchanging phone numbers both departed. Victoria got on the bus for Mumbai returning back home and Robert returned back to his hometown Chandigarh.

Victoria reached home, this time she was feeling more confident about herself. She decided as she had enough money now to get her dad operated and start some small scale business that would earn her family a livelihood. She opened a milk business and started going for milk arrival deliveries from 3 am in the morning. She appointed two boys for milk delivery purposes. Two months passed by, and the business did not give many results but it was difficult to carry on with the milk business as it was too early in the morning.

Victoria and Robert were in touch with each other on phone, this was the time when mobile phones were just launched in India on a wider scale. They spoke to each other almost every day. Victoria liked cycling, every evening while talking to Robert. She cycled almost 10 km every day. Victor and Kenny were recovering from their illness slowly and were coming back to normal health. One night, when everyone was sitting for dinner, after having a few bites, suddenly Victoria's dad complained of heart pain, Victoria asked, "Dad are you alright, should we go to the doctor now?" But Victor couldn't utter a word. She left eating and rushed to the hospital and admitted him but soon as the doctor checked him, He said, "Victor had a severe heart attack due to which his heart stopped working." Victor was declared to be dead by the doctor's team.

In 2003 on 28 September, he passed away at the age of 43 years. Victoria was 20 years old, Kenny was weeping terribly hearing Victor is dead, she shouted aloud, "Why did you leave now when you started improving?" Victoria informed all the extended family members about the sudden demise of her father. Everybody visited Victoria's house for condolence. Victor's Mother, brother and sisters wept sitting next to Victor's dead body. According to Hindu tradition, the last rituals of a man or woman are carried out by the elder son, but Victor had no son but only two daughters and as Victoria was elder, she carried out all the final rituals of her dad with some family members, mainly dad's sisters' son and his wife who helped her at least in this situation. Funeral's cremation activity "Agni" was performed by Victor's sisters' son. Everyone showed their concern and condolence towards Victor but no one asked whether the family needed any help and thus departed from there.

After paying all hospital bills, funeral bills and milk business investments, she had a good amount of money which her mother Kenny decided to invest into gold, saying it would help later.

Victoria was now free from her dad's operation responsibility, now she had her sister and mother to look after. Robert visited Mumbai with two of his friends, Victoria helped them explore Mumbai. Then after a few months, he called Victoria to visit Chandigarh. Victoria visited Chandigarh and spent a good time with Robert, discovering each other more. Victoria was planning what business she could start as a milk business did not work well and it was hectic too. She started learning four-wheeler driving at the driving school and within three months she became an excellent driver.

Robert started asking Victoria to marry him, but Victoria refused the proposal because she knew the struggles she went through and she never wanted to disclose it to Robert. She didn't want to make it complicated but Robert kept on convincing her to marry him. After a few months, Robert convinced her to meet his parents. Victoria agreed to host the family for lunch. Robert's family came from Chandigarh to meet Victoria. Robert's family had two younger brothers, a father and a mother. While on the way to visit her home, Robert called Victoria to ask for her finger's ring size, Victoria was afraid and out of curiosity she asked Robert, "Why do you need my ring size?" Robert said, "We will be having a small engagement ceremony at home." Victoria was shocked to hear that as it was a lifetime commitment and Robert was unaware of her past, but then she thought he was a good guy to spend life with, let's get engaged after a year or two they will get married. Soon after this news, Victoria arranged a small hotel banquet hall for her engagement ceremony.

She informed her relatives although they were not of any use to her as a family in past situations but then too she had to inform them about her engagement ceremony as informed during her dad's funeral. After All, they needed to know that Victoria was getting engaged. Robert's family visited Victoria's house at 1 pm. All of them were happy, her sister Princess was excited that Victoria would be getting married now, Robert's father seemed to be a gentleman and her mother was like all mothers while his brother seemed to be well qualified. They all spent a good time interacting with each other and left for the ring ceremony which took place at a banquet hall in a hotel in presence of relatives and friends.

Victoria was overthinking, "Is it good to get engaged to Robert without him knowing her past childhood and teenage?" She was with the quilt, was she taking the right decision, then she thought, after all, it was past and circumstances turned out to be different for her from other normal girls. She assured herself that nothing can go wrong and that the choice she made to be Robert's partner in her future life was correct. She could relive her life to the fullest with a loving partner like Robert and she could pursue her dreams. She will have her own support system in the form of Robert and his family. After the engagement ceremony family returned home, Robert's father proposed marriage after 2 months, but Victoria did not agree to it and asked for 2 years at least for marriage to take place, in order to establish herself completely before marriage because she was the only source of income to her family.

Destiny had different plans, Robert and his family compelled Victoria to get married in 2 months as they said, "There shouldn't be more time gap between engagement and marriage." Victoria thought it was God's decision and accepted the proposal. As the jewellery was already in stock. Marriage expenses had to the taken care of. Robert's mother had demanded clothes for the entire elaborated family as a gift, nothing except this. Victoria, Princess and Mom started with the preparation of marriage by shopping for the wedding and as the wedding has to be conducted in Mumbai, booking banquet and caterers along with the cards and all the work required for the wedding. All the *baraati's* from groom's family came all the way from Chandigarh around 30 people from the groom's side and 60 people from the bride's side attended the wedding. It was a beautifully planned wedding in a hotel banquet with all the arrangements done by Victoria. As the wedding began and when the groom and bride were supposed to take their vows. The manager of banquet caterers interrupted to speak to Victoria. Victoria thought in her mind "What's wrong now?" but he said, "50 plates will be extra," as the number of guests increased.

Victoria agreed to pay the extra bill. The wedding took place in Robert's family's traditional manner. After the wedding was completed all the guests started departing slowly, groom's side guest went to a hotel stay which was arranged by Victoria. Victoria, Princess and her mother returned home. Vidai ceremony was on the next morning, Victoria had to leave Mumbai as well as Princess and Mom alone in Mumbai. She was upset as well as happy that her struggles were now over. She will have a new family new people new beginning. Victoria left with Robert and his family to Chandigarh. Victoria had mistaken that Robert was from Chandigarh, Robert was from a small village in western Uttar Pradesh. Newly wedded Victoria and Robert spent their first night in the first-class compartment of a train. Robert and Victoria were talking to each other sitting on the train, suddenly a phone rang, it was Princess on the other side, crying and weeping that she was left alone, somehow Victoria convinced her not to worry she will be visiting her shortly and will speak to her daily and she will be taken care off and reminded her to study well. It was their first-night being married, they had good quality time. The next morning, the train reached Delhi station and from Delhi, the journey to Robert's house in the village was 4 hrs away.

Big vehicles came to pick up the family, it was the month of January, which is the coldest month in the northern region. By evening 7 pm Victoria and family reached Robert's house in a village where there was a huge crowd waiting for their welcome. As the couple got out of the car, they were welcomed by the people, ladies singing songs and music playing.

Winters are chilly in the North. Victoria was shivering due to the cold and surprised to see so many people around her, women were jumping on her to see her face. Victoria was asked to cover her face with *ghoonghat* by Robert. It seemed to be their tradition, so Victoria was in *ghoonghat* women pounding on her just to see her face. Victoria started feeling very special. There was a small function where all the women sat together and sang songs, one by one opened her *ghoonghat* and gave her blessing and money as well. Victoria enjoyed the ceremony then she was made to sing the song before the ceremony ended. Victoria refused earlier than Sang "Om Jai Jagdish Hare" to conclude the ceremony. All the guests left for home and Victoria and Robert were given their sweet room. Victoria and Robert had a conversation about the culture in the village. It was all very new to Victoria and amazingly surprising. Victoria had come from a very different and open background, unaware of the customs and traditions of Robert's family. She started thinking what if these people come to know about her past, how they would react. She came to know she was a daughter in law to a big and known family. She was busy thinking over and over, Listening to Robert's village culture, then suddenly Robert kissed her and hugged her and the love time began. They made passionate and magical love and had delightful sex till 4 am in the morning and went to sleep by 5 am. Next-day morning Robert's mother, Mia knocked on the door, with her two sisters. Victoria got ready, they helped her to wear her saree and jewellery. Victoria was wondering morning 9 am, they are getting her ready with saree. ll they said was how this was the culture of in the village where women will come, pick up her *ghoonghat,* seeing her face and giving blessing gifts will be carried on throughout the day. Women came blessed Victoria and left. This continued for the entire day, some women also, asked Victoria to speak in *'madrasi' language.* Victoria said, "I am Marathi, not madrasi," At that time she got to know the ignorance of the people staying in that village. They said they don't speak any other language, all women with *ghoonghat* sitting around. Victoria then thought she was not special. It was not special. It was the culture in the village to always have *ghoonghat* for women, only aged women were without ghoonghat but pallu on the head. This "Muh - dikhai" tradition continued for 5 days. Victoria's reception ceremony was planned for the next day. Victoria's mother and sister Princess visited Delhi and then reached the village at evening 5 pm.

There was a huge open garden ceremony planned by Robert's father. Approximately 12000 people attended the reception ceremony. It was a grand occasion for the entire village, everyone was present there. Princess and Victoria's mom was happy to see Victoria happy. The next day Victoria, Princess and mom left for Mumbai for their one more tradition called "Patphere". Where the bride returns home and the husband comes to receive her after a few days. Victoria had never thought she would get such good people in her new family, she was really happy. Victoria and her family returned back to Mumbai. She stayed in Mumbai for a few days learning to drive for some time. One day, Robert came to receive her to take her back home. The couple went back to their house in a village in Western Uttar Pradesh. Slowly staying in the village, Victoria started getting bored, as there was nothing to do in the village. Women were not allowed to go out of the house and she had to carry *ghoonghat* on her head at least throughout the day. She found out within a couple of months that society here was male-dominated, women were not allowed to have their point of view or opinions, and women were only found cooking or taking care of animals, cows and buffaloes for milk. Male used to work at the farms. Men in the village ate non-veg but women were all vegetarians. It was difficult for Victoria to spend time in the village. Robert had promised Victoria to stay in Chandigarh or any metro city before marriage. She was guilty that how will she help her sister and mom with their living. She was so depressed day by day in the village, that she would start to cry with sunset and could hardly hold on to it by 9 pm. It became her daily routine to cry in the evening, as she couldn't find out what was next.

How she could establish herself to help her family. Days went by and whatever money her family had were all spent on Princess and mom's daily essentials, rent, bills, and her mom's fissure and fistula complications also increased. Victoria couldn't wait for more but asked for help from Robert. Robert agreed to help Victoria's family financially. But at that time Robert was jobless too. In spite of having a big house and big cars, he was not earning enough. Victoria gave her mother whatever jewellery they had made, in order to meet daily needs. After a few days, Victoria tried to convince Robert to shift to some city so that both could earn something by starting their venture on a small scale. But Robert was with the mindset like all the orthodox villager's mindset that women shouldn't go out of the house. She realized she was a part of a completely male-dominated society. Victoria was taking contraceptive pills at that time to avoid pregnancy but when her mother-in-law came to know about it, she started telling Victoria to stop taking the pills, or she can't be a mother later on. Continuously nagging behind her and so understanding her Victoria stopped the pills.

Mia asked Victoria to give whatever jewellery she got from the groom's family. Victoria agreed and gave back her gold jewellery which was a gift from Robert's close relatives. And now onwards slowly arguments started between the family. Victoria realized it was going to be difficult for her. Roberts's behaviour also changed. Robert often went to his friend's house in the village to play cards and pass his time, leaving Victoria alone at home, he would only come home for food. When asked by Victoria, "Robert, why you have to be at your friends' house the entire day, I am bored at home." Robert would say, "I get bored at home too, so I go to them." And when Victoria asked, "What should I do the entire day?" He said "You are a woman, you cook and stay at home quietly." Victoria was upset by his behaviour, she found out that she had married someone from the ancient era. He was found angry and frustrated most of the time on silly things like there is no salt in dal or curd is sourer, or his shirt is not properly ironed by Victoria, any small meaningless reason was enough for him to get angry. But Victoria and Robert's sex life was sparky and satisfying, in spite of arguments between them.

IT ISN'T OVER YET!

One fine day, Victoria noticed that she missed her periods. After visiting the doctor, it was clear that Victoria was pregnant. Victoria was clueless now, what was her life going to be. She was going to be a mother. Was she really prepared for it? She was 21 years old, but her past didn't allow her to be a mother. She was totally confused. After 3 months of pregnancy, in sonography done it was cleared that it was a girl child growing in Victoria's womb. She was more terrified after getting that news, as being a girl, she knew what hell she had been through since a little girl. She knew it was difficult to survive as a girl from her bad past experiences like molestation from her uncle, uncle's friend, rape by a neighbour.

She can't think of anything bad happening to her daughter. She started convincing Robert to abort the baby. She was not ready to give birth, but couldn't explain to him in detail about the past as she was hiding that since they met. She called her family doctor in Mumbai, asking that she is 3 months pregnant and it is a girl child and she wanted to abort it. Doctor convinced Victoria that "You are a woman, you can't take away a girl child's life like this being yourself a woman, it's harsh and bad mentality. Be a human." She was already in the fifth month of her pregnancy and did not have the courage to terminate her baby. Victoria somehow convinced herself and promised to be a good mother in a time that was coming for her next. Robert never visited the Doctor along with Victoria. She was sent for routine check-ups with some of the family, friends, or a member of his village. Victoria found it weird that Robert's behaviour changed and approached her differently. He never spent time with her.

Victoria's health started falling down as a part of the pregnancy process which all women go through nausea, vomiting, morning sickness and mostly laid in bed. Watching movies and keeping herself engaged without getting any negative thoughts into her mind, waiting to welcome the newborn and the day arrived when the labour pain started and Victoria was taken to the hospital. After 7 hours of labour pain, Victoria delivered a beautiful adorable package of love, her baby girl. She was named Darbie by her grandfather. When she touched her for the first time, she promised herself, "I will protect my daughter from the world, no matter what comes my way." The world had been harsh for her. That mother's powerful emotion was now developed in Victoria's heart and mind, she had become a warrior now.

Victoria stayed in the hospital for a few days and was soon discharged to go home. Victoria returned home to the village along with her dear daughter Darbie and Robert. Victoria was a woman now who was in charge of a little baby. Victoria was more engaged and concentrated on Darbie, taking care of her baby was life for her now. Princess visited the village to meet Darbie for the very first time. Victoria was happy to see Princess, as she was grown up now and was about to clear the 12th board examination. Victoria was at peace of mind that her dreams are coming in regard to Princess. After a week Victoria, Princess and Darbie came to Mumbai. It was Darbie's first air travel when she was 2 months old. Victoria's mother was happy to see her home with Darbie. Victoria continued her driving practice during that time. It was always in her mind, what will she tell her daughter about her mother's education, she had left her studies in the 10th class before exams. She asked Princess if she can study further? Princess replied, "Of course, I will fill the form tomorrow." So she decided to appear for the 10th board exam as an external student.

She filled up the form for the examination and started preparing for it along with taking care of her daughter Darbie. After 3 months she went back to the village. Initially, Robert appeared to be very happy, he took good care of Darbie and Victoria. It was constantly going on in Victoria's mind about Darbie's future education. As staying in a village wouldn't have that many opportunities for Darbie to excel. Girls were never allowed to go out of the house or speak to anyone, it was completely a male-dominated society. Victoria tried to convince Robert to move out of the village and stay in some city. As Victoria's mom and sister Princess were in Mumbai, Victoria decided to start a new life in Mumbai. Robert however did not agree, and the arguments and fights started between the two resulting in physical abuse for Victoria. He slapped Victoria straight on her face, Victoria was shattered to see how Robert treated her. She was emotionally shattered. As Robert was jobless at that time, his mind was empty and we all know an empty mind is a devil's workshop. Robert had to support Victoria's family as well as his own so he asked for help from his father. Mr Samuel was this gentlemen who went out of his way to help Victoria's family financially.

Mr Samuel decided on a fixed amount to be given to Victoria's family for their living and asked the couple to go and stay in Mumbai for a few months, Victoria shifted to Mumbai with Darbie and Robert and they rented an apartment 30 km away from Victoria's maiden family. It was a new beginning for Victoria and Robert as a nuclear family with their little daughter Darbie. Robert's father deposited funds every month for their living. Robert was jobless. Robert did not find Mumbai happening, as he was born and bought up in a village he was unable to adjust to the atmosphere of a city. He was bored of staying in Mumbai. Robert used to consume marijuana very often, Victoria was unaware of this addiction of Robert. Robert left for the village after every small interval.

He sent his grandfather to stay in Mumbai with Victoria and Darbie and he himself stayed in village. Victoria appeared for her class 10th board examination and passed the exams. Now, Victoria was thinking of doing some sort of course which could help her financially. She enrolled herself on the medical transcription programme and joined the course. She started studying again. Robert was done with Mumbai, so he went back to his village. Whereas Victoria and Darbie stayed back for the completion of the course.

One fine day, when Victoria was in class suddenly Robert visited her from his village. She was delighted to see Robert back but as they reached home. He behaved so badly with her, abusing her and tearing the white shirt she was wearing. He started with doubts about her fidelity because she was wearing a shirt and going to classes. He was of a stereotype mindset about women's outfits. He judged all the women depending on their outfits. Victoria was crying. She did call her father in law Mr Samuel to complain about Robert's behaviour. After a few days, Robert realised his mistake but the difference of opinion was always there between the two. After a few months Robert, Victoria and Darbie shifted to Jaipur. As his father in law Mr Samuel had bought a new house for Robert and his family. After shifting to Jaipur, Darbie was 3 years old and started going to playschool.

After a few months, the entire family visited the village for Diwali. Everyone enjoyed their festival in the village with all their customs and traditions. The next day, one of the villagers in the neighbourhood visited Victoria and had a newspaper in hand. After reading the newspaper, Victoria was surprisingly shocked to read that Robert's father, Mr Samuel was the godfather of that state as well as the most wanted criminal in that area, he was the 'Don'. Victoria was lost to hear that such a great gentleman with such a big heart and good behaviour, 'How could he be a Don?' So, Victoria confronted Robert regarding this, where Robert explained, "Yes, my father is a real don and godfather of Western Uttar Pradesh." Now, Victoria was again clueless about where she had landed finally.

Everything seemed unreal to her. She was the daughter-in-law to the don of that state. She was in acute shockut it didn't bother her much, as her life was going on smoothly so far. After a few days, Robert's family left for Jaipur. Initially, Robert behaved good but slowly he was seen getting addicted to marijuana. He was jobless in Jaipur too, he used to visit the village very often, leaving Victoria and Darbie with his oarents. Whenever Victoria asked, "Why you are smoking marijuana daily?" He replied, "It is none of your business, you and your family is looked after well, so my mind your own things." Fights and arguments had started between the couple. Robert convinced Victoria that marijuana is nothing but a simple herb that is consumed by the people of his village and also used in many medicines as a drug, it is completely harmless and asked her to try it.

Victoria agreed to it and took the first puff, then the second and then every day before sex they consumed it. Victoria found it good, as for some time she would completely forget her past and live fully in present. One day a phone rang, Victoria answered it, it was some policeman on the other side inquiring about her father-in-law, Mr Samuel. She immediately informed her father-in-law about the phone call. At that time her in-laws stayed in the village. One day, Robert went on a trip with some of his friends, saying a lie at home, that he is going for some business meeting to start a new venture. But actually went for a fun trip with his so-called friend Suzuki who was a 30-year-old girl from Israel. Robert took her to Agra to see the famous Taj Mahal and then to Udaipur on a jungle safari. They had a good time with her, he lied to Victoria that "I am going on a business trip with friends." This news broke Victoria completely. When she read Robert and Suzuki's love messages on his phone. She went to Mumbai for a few days with Darbie when Robert was in the village. Victoria was happy to be home after a long time. Princess had passed her 12th board examination with flying colours and was seeking admission into Engineering College. Victoria was very happy for her sister, sounded like she had made it. Victoria and Princess were shopping in a mall, where they met Victoria's ex-boyfriend Cavin. The one who stole the scooty parts and things from Victoria's house but Victoria had forgotten about all that. They went on talking, as he too was married now. Victoria was tense due to Robert's behaviour, she spoke to her ex regarding this. He said everything will be fine, this happens between every couple. We decided to meet again for a buzz. Cavin was very funny by nature; he cracked so many jokes that Victoria wouldn't stop laughing.

After a few drinks and a long talk, both parted their way home. A few days later Victoria was back in Jaipur where her father-in-law asked her to sell the flat he purchased for them. Victoria was in search of a flat buyer now. Robert was back from the village. Robert and Victoria started living happily with each other, after a couple of months, Victoria again missed her periods. She was pregnant again. This time was very difficult for the couple. As both were jobless, monthly expenses were provided by her father-in-law. Victoria then thought that there might be some family business through which Mr Samuel contributed to their living as well as Robert's brother's expenses. This time too Victoria went to doctor alone again, Robert never accompanied her anywhere even to the routine doctor check-up. After a few days again, he went back to the village therefore Victoria also visited Mumbai with Darbie and was 6 months pregnant. Her mom Kenny wanted Victoria to be blessed with a son this time, so as per the suggestion by one of her friends, they decided to visit one temple in Gujarat. Victoria had already purchased one four-wheeler in case of emergency and for Princess to learn and travel in Mumbai. Kenny suggested she go by train, but Victoria decided to take a car drive from temple to Gujarat. She still was in the condition of being six months pregnant, so she decided to drive but as she was an excellent driver, it didn't matter to her. All started their journey to temple in a car with Victoria as the driver. It was a wonderful trip. They covered a distance of 490 km within 10 hours. They reached the temple safely.

As per Kenny's wish, prayed to God for a male child this time, they stayed in a hotel for one night and started the next morning back to Mumbai. They reached home back in Mumbai safe and secure. Victoria returned back to Jaipur with Darbie. The delivery time was coming closer, Victoria had made a good social circle in the Jaipur society, she had friends to go around, for walks, and for kitty tea parties. This time the kitty party was planned at Victoria's house, she ordered some snacks for her friends, as she was a cleanliness freak she cleaned the complete house thoroughly well. She had completed her 8 months of pregnancy. A kitty party was planned for 4 pm, one friend arrived at her place. She was alone at home with Darbie, as her father-in-law had left in the morning itself and her brother-in-law went for a movie. Robert and his mother were in the village. As Victoria sat on the couch to chat with a friend, another friend came, and when she got up to welcome her, she saw that her dress and couch were wet. Her water bag had burst. Friends suggested her to call the doctor immediately and the doctor asked her to get admitted to the hospital for delivery immediately. Her friend insisted and accompanied her to the hospital. Her father-in-law was informed so he took a U-turn back to the hospital after hearing the news. Robert and his mother Mia also started from the village, and

Victoria's mother Kenny started from Mumbai to Jaipur. After injecting artificial pains for 8 hours, Victoria delivered a cute little baby boy at 2 am. She was conscious before she handed her baby to any of the family members. As soon as she was out, she saw her brother-in-law was present in the hospital. She handed over the baby to him to take care of in his presence as well as nurses. Then, she was unconscious for an hour.

When she woke up she found her mother, Robert and Robert's mother around her. She was happy to see them all. Victoria was again a mother of a newborn. Everyone was happy to welcome the newborn. He was named Derrick by her mother-in-law Mia. After a few days, she was discharged home. She had got a fully busy schedule for her, as Darbie started with her grade 1 studies. Victoria didn't have any time to think about anything, she wanted her children to be scholars in studies. Darbie's academics were good since childhood as Victoria devoted most of the time studying with Darbie. She neglected the little one, as she was breastfeeding the second one, so she could hardly complete her sleep. Her health started deteriorating and her blood pressure started falling down. After medication, she was better. Victoria was searching for a buyer to sell that house as asked by Mr Samuel. This time she had the responsibility of selling that house. Victoria found the buyer and sold the flat with Mr Samuel's support. Instead of helping Victoria to shift to the next rented flat in the same society, Robert went on a trip with his friends. Victoria had to do all the shifting work all alone with little kids. Robert never took responsibility like a father or a partner and never assisted her in any of housework.

BACK TO SQUARE ONE

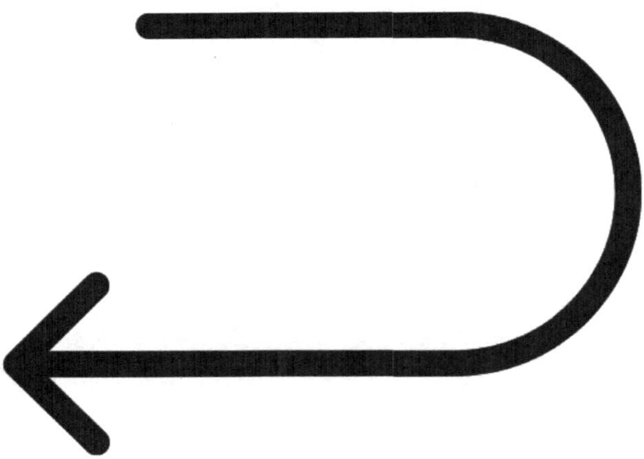

After Darbies' school session was over, Victoria shifted to Chandigarh with Robert and two children. Again, it was a new beginning for Victoria with two children, as the little one started crawling it became more difficult for Victoria to take care of both. Victoria's mother suggested that she would keep Darbie in Mumbai for one year. Victoria agreed and sent Darbie to Mumbai to stay with Princess and Kenny. Robert's father had opened a new venture of the printing press for Robert in partnership with his friend, where Mr Samuel invested all the money and his friend was a working partner. Without talking to Robert, he never wanted third-person influence in his business too, where he knew nothing about the printing press. He never wanted it, this way. Then too Robert started working in that printing press against his desire. One year passed by, Victoria's son Derrick was 1.5 years old now, she was missing Darbie, so she asked Princess to drop Darbie back in Chandigarh. Princess had started further studies as a student of B.E. Princess dropped Darbie to Chandigarh and went back to Mumbai. A few months passed by Darbie had started her schooling in one of the best schools in Chandigarh and her son Derrick also started going to playschool. One fine day, Victoria again found love messages on Robert's phone. When she was reading it, suddenly Robert came and started fighting with her, beating and abusing her. It was his fault, but he was beating Victoria badly. That her eye had swollen and were bruises all over her body. Victoria was heartbroken and depressed again "Why is this happening to her?" Victoria and Robert had a very good love and sexual relationship. The only thing missing was Robert's responsibility as a father and a husband but Victoria was good enough to manage all responsibilities of her children and house. She was always a steadfast person. A giver always whether it is love, care, or dedication towards family and humanity. She never expected infidelity from Robert, never. Victoria lost her trust in Robert, And fights became big and big like monsters she never expected to be.

Robert and Victoria started hurting each other verbally. Robert accused Victoria of being the worst mistake of his life. She was shattered by his ill-treatment towards her. Marijuana was consumed by both on daily basis, which never led them to skip their sexual intimacy every night. Throughout the day they had fights and arguments, but during the night they were in each other's arms. Robert started with domestic violence very often. Every time some part of Victoria's body was damaged or bruised but somehow beating did not affect Victoria as since childhood she was prone to physical abuse.

He started insulting and doubting her infidelity. Victoria was innocent, but at the same time carried the guilt of her past which was hidden from Robert. Both the kids were terrified looking at their father hitting their mother every day. Victoria believed that the cycle of her father is repeating again but the difference was that financially they were stable because of her father-in-law, Mr Samuel's grace. Robert started visiting the village often like earlier he used to go. Victoria stayed alone with Darbie and Derrick most of the time. Sometimes father-in-law, sometimes mother-in-law stayed with her. Robert was engaged with his new friends who wanted to start a new venture in the e-commerce industry. He opened a new office with them with all investments from his pocket, there was no financial investment from his friends. It was a risky project.

Victoria thought he was improving in responsibilities, but at the same time, there was a fear in her mind about the loss in business as

Robert was completely unaware of the e-commerce industry. Victoria engaged herself in reading books, she would complete 1 book within 10 days, taking care of kids and the house, whatever time she had, she read books and made some good friends circle as it was a good army society. After a few days, Robert discovered that his friends only learnt from that business, with complete loss financially. He had been cheated in business and he suffered financial loss. Day by day, he became short-tempered, always pissed off at every little thing in the house in regards to less salt in food, no clothes, not ironed properly and any other silly reasons. He started bursting out at Victoria. Both kids were terrified watching his behaviour. Kids developed a fear against Robert and sympathy and hatred towards Victoria as she can't help herself from his beatings. Victoria found herself as she was at the age of 8 years when her father used to abuse her badly. She started going into depression and that was the time when she developed the habit of reading books, by reading stories of others, she used to forget about herself, was so engrossed in reading that her problems appeared to be nothing. Both kids were growing up, she was very particular about their academics and sports as well as inculcating moral values toward humanity in her children. Of course, she was the cleanliness freak. Most of her time was spent either with kids, cleaning or reading. She was the one who was completely responsible for taking care of the children and the house. She managed it very well as guided by Robert, whatever amount of money she got every month, she used as per the choice of the family, type of food, clothes, lifestyle as the kids and Robert wanted. She was from a humble family, had not much idea about lifestyles, learning from society and friends. She gave the best lifestyle she could for that amount of money.

Robert didn't have a job or business. He didn't go out of the house for work but only went out to chill with friends. He knew he was doing nothing as a partner or father, but never accepted it and nor tried to change but instead took out his frustration towards Victoria. Robert's temper had increased and he started beating his daughter 'Darbie' for silly reasons, like once he asked her "Darbie dear, please give me half glass of water". Darbie went and got a full glass of water, seeing a full glass of water, he burst on her saying "When I asked for half glass of water, how can you give me a full glass, you don't listen to me." And slapped her. There was not any strong reason for him to beat Darbie or Victoria, very small negligible reasons were enough, for him to go violent, and when Victoria came in between when Darbie was beaten, she was beaten along with her. The situation now was worsening.. So now when Robert's father came to know about his condition of Robert. He decided to shift Robert and Victoria's family, to a place called Muzzaffarnagar city which was 20 minutes' distance from their village but was a city. Robert's father took this decision so that the family would stay closer to him as he stayed in the village during that time. Princess had completed her education and was working as a Software Engineer in a renowned multinational company. Victoria was at ease from her side now, she was proud that Princess made her dream come true. She was capable of taking care of herself and her mother. It was a proud and memorable moment for Victoria. Victoria visited Mumbai with Darbie and Derrick.

After spending a few days with Princess, Victoria discovered that Princess had been dating a guy named Racheal who was from South Kerala. When she met Racheal, she was pleased to meet a well-qualified, responsible, good looking man with high aspirations. She was proud of the choice of partner Princess selected to marry. After a formal meeting with Racheal's family, the wedding was planned according to mutual convenience. The wedding took place in the hometown of Racheal. In Kerela, where all the wedding expenses were paid by Racheal's family. Victoria's Father-in-law contributed financially helping Victoria to carry out the Reception ceremony which was planned in Mumbai. Mr Samuel, with one of his friends and his daughter, Robert and Victoria's family, attended the wedding in Kerala. The "kanyadaan" ceremony was performed by Robert and Victoria. Victoria was the happiest person now, as she had completed all her responsibilities towards her sister. She was in relief. The reception ceremony took place in a beautiful huge hotel banquet hall in Mumbai in the presence of the bride and groom's friends and relatives, with all expenses done from the Bride's side. It was the best and happiest day of Victoria's life.

Victoria and her family left-back for Muzaffarnagar, as kids' schools, were supposed to start soon. "Muzzaffarnagar" one more place added to Victoria's journey. Darbie and Derrick had a new school, new friends and a new atmosphere. But father's temperament was the same pissed-off all the time. They were afraid to talk to him. Kids only followed whatever was told by their father. Victoria was calming her mind by reading books. In a year, Princess and Racheal shifted to Bangalore as they got bigger opportunities to excel. They lived happily with each other. Victoria was busy with kids, academics, a new set of friends around her, but her mind always had one doubt in her head since they were living in Jaipur, that Robert must be married to some other girl as well because he never stayed continuously with her for one year. He constantly kept on visiting the village for 2 months or so.

Robert's violent behaviour was proof whenever he was asked any question about himself. He always told Victoria not to call him when he was out of the house, he never answered where, why, and how questions by Victoria about him. Day by day, this doubt started growing. Now, as Robert was in his city. After all his father was a godfather and don of that city. He became more powerful but at the same time more violent. After 2 years of marriage, Princess delivered her very own bundle of joy. A cute, beautiful, adorable little baby princess named Aayara. As soon as Victoria heard this news, she immediately left from Muzaffarnagar with Robert to welcome the newborn. When Victoria saw Aayara for the first time, she felt like some magical powers came into her hands. One more girl child was into her world. She thought, "Now, I am the mother of 2 daughters, it's my responsibility to protect them against evil and guide them in future with the help of my past bad experiences." She determined herself to be the best mother and aunt to an adorably cute baby from the heaven of God. After spending some time with the newborn, Victoria and Robert left back home.

Victoria was busy again with the kids and reading. Robert's behaviour was sometimes good and sometimes worst. Domestic violence was so high this time Victoria was left with broken bones, a fractured and bruised body. Robert created this same domestic violence against Darbie as well. Now, Darbie was a little girl who was beaten so badly on her butt by a belt that she couldn't sit in the classroom due to her swollen butt. It was a painful time for her. Victoria started cursing herself for giving Darbie such kind of life, where it seems Victoria's childhood was repeated by physical abuse to Darbie. Domestic violence increased day by day, after every violent incident, Robert used to apologize to Victoria and Darbie saying "I won't repeat it again, please forgive me."

Robert's violent behaviour had become his habit. Robert had helped Victoria's family financially and also Victoria was guilty that her past was hidden from him. She forgave him every time, she suffered violence. Victoria started asking for separation as it was now getting difficult to stay with Robert, he was continuously hitting her and daughter Darbie. She wanted to save her daughter from Robert's beatings but was unable to stop him. Watching Robert's behaviour his son was so afraid of him, that he began crying whenever his name was called by his father. No liberty to speak, no liberty to do anything in that house, had to follow Robert's instructions only. Life became hell for Victoria and the kids. Darbie was studying in grade 6 and her son was in grade 1. All three were fed up with Robert's behaviour. Victoria and Darbie decided to run out of the house. As Darbie suggested she run away she remembered how Victoria had convinced her mother to run away from the house and how they escaped. It was history repeating itself for Victoria.

Annual Academics result day was coming near. All three planned to escape from the house on that day after collecting results from school. Victoria had already applied for a transfer certificate from school. They started packing everyday little bit whenever Robert went out of the house. All the clothes, shoes, stationery, toys, and a total of 13 bags were packed and kept in the storeroom and the result day arrived. As soon as Robert left out of the house for his work. Victoria immediately booked an SUV car for their journey, with all their luggage of 13 bags they reached school, collected results from the school and started for Delhi. Victoria had only 700 rupees in her pocket when she started from home. She had to arrange money by selling some gold earrings in Delhi, so she could reach Mumbai. After 4 hours they reached Delhi to one of her friends named Shez who became friends with Victoria when she stayed in Chandigarh earlier, she was her neighbour.

She got down at Shez's house and explained the situation and asked for help to accompany her in order to sell gold rings and arrange money for fare to reach Mumbai. She agreed to help Victoria. They left the kids at Shez house with her daughter and went to a jewellery shop where they sold the gold rings and got money. Victoria decided to travel the next day to Mumbai by train, as there was a lot of luggage. Actually, Victoria also felt that if Robert realizes his mistake, he would come to take her and the kids back home. When Robert returned home, he found that no one was in the house, he started calling Victoria. But Victoria was so scared to answer his calls that she kept on disconnecting them. After some time she forwarded the handwritten note that she had written for her in-laws, where she mentioned she is leaving Robert, for the kid's better future and don't want anything from him. After reading the note her in-laws called her. She spoke to them and told them she was in Delhi at a friend's house and will go to Mumbai the next day. Her father-in-law was upset with this act by Victoria, as she left her house without informing them. Victoria apologized for the sudden flight from the house. She thought if Robert realizes his mistake he would change and come to pick her up by the next day, as now he knew where she was staying in Delhi. Victoria had a couple of beer cans with her friend Shez talking all about the present situation of her life.

The night passed by and the arrival day came, the train was scheduled on time. They left Shez house to the railway station, Victoria in her head she thought that Robert didn't actually love her or her kids, he never wanted them back in his life. According to her doubt about his, another marriage appeared to be true, as he didn't come to take them back. Now she was sure Robert didn't want her. The train journey started. This time Victoria was again ready for a new challenge being not a teenager but a mother of two as a warrior. The next day train arrived at Mumbai station. Victoria's mother Kenny had gone to Bangalore to visit her sister Princess, to help her out with her baby care. Victoria and the kids reached their Mumbai rented 1 BHK flat where the key was kept with a neighbour. They opened the door and moved inside. Kids were so happy and excited to start a new life without Robert their so-called Dad. Now, Victoria was under deep stress about what should be her next step. The first thing in the morning, she did was visit a jewellery shop and sell some of her mom's jewellery so that she can raise some funds. She gathered 4 lacs rupees. Now schools had been started for Mumbai kids. She got her kids admitted to one of the best schools in that area. During the process of admission, she processed requests for Aadhar cards and purchased books and uniforms for kids. Darbie and Derrick were excited to go to a new school. They started going to school. Victoria planned everything well. Looked upon kids' academies and sports, cooking for them. Now she was mom and dad both for kids, sometimes strict, sometimes lenient. She started to live again without any abuse, 3 months passed by. There was a question, what's next, what she would do to earn her living, as she was hardly qualified, she wasn't able to find a job for her.

BE STRONG, BE YOU!

After applying at many places for jobs, she got an opportunity to be an insurance agent, which you know, everyone gets when you start hunting for jobs. She did the complete course, appeared for the insurance examination and cleared it, but could not approach anyone for the insurance client. Knowing her past she hesitated to talk to strangers so never excelled in this insurance agent field. She wasn't able to figure out which job she could do. Though an enlightenment happened and she realized, she was a very good driver. So she attempted to interview the lady cab driving community which she passed and started driving for it. But it was difficult for her to take care of her children and her full-time cab driver job. Few days passed by, but it didn't work longer as kids were neglected due to her work. Victoria was missing Robert as well, day by day. After all, they loved each other and had a very good relationship.

Victoria thought over and over and decided to visit Robert once again by leaving her kids with her mom. As she entered Robert's house, he was happy to see her. They just hugged each other forgetting past and had good sex and food and started their conversation about all the things that happened in her life since she left Robert.

Victoria convinced Robert to send monthly expenses to look after the kids as she was not able to make enough money to maintain the kid's lifestyle. They decided that Victoria, Darbie and their son would stay in Mumbai for their children's better future, wherein Robert would visit them as per his time. Victoria approached her father-in-law to lend some amount of money so that she could start a small scale cloud kitchen or restaurant business. But he did not agree to it. Victoria returned back to Mumbai. Robert visited them after a year with his father Mr Samuel, All were happy to see them.

Kids saw some amount of positive change in Roberts's behaviour. They enjoyed Robert's company for that 15-20 days. Robert had clear instructions to Victoria not to call directly on his phone without intimating him on WhatsApp ping. It was weird but this gave Victoria a clear idea that her doubt about his other marriage was right to some extent. She was confused but never had approached to find out the truth. She didn't have anyone to support her to find out whether Robert was married to someone or not. Victoria hardly spoke to people. Once she asked her mother-in-law about it sarcastically and even she replied, "If he is married then, what? You are been taken care of financially, why do you have to worry? Just take care of your kids." It was pretty much clear that she was never going to say anything directly, with all the chaos in mind, life was going on for Victoria. Children were growing up. She was engaged in kids and reading. Robert sometimes called in a week sometimes in 10 days, he hardly spoke to Victoria and the kids. Victoria started feeling lonely and left out especially when she found friends around her with their spouses.

She made new friends in society, started cycling and running and started taking care of herself and tried to stop smoking. Most of the time Victoria was in a destructive state of mind as she was left alone after kids were busy in their schools and activities, she wanted to do something but couldn't find out what and how. It was a situation where she was clear she didn't want to stay with Robert for a long time because when Robert visited them for a short duration his behaviour was better than staying for long. It was clear they won't be able to stay together forever. Slowly life became monotonous for her. In spite of her kids around her, she started falling down, went into depression and her smoking increased. Kids tried to stop Victoria from falling apart but

Victoria couldn't help the thought process going on in her mind about the life which she experienced. She had never hurt anyone, then why she was chosen to suffer like this, was Robert really married? This thought never left her mind. In spite of asking directly about his other marriage to him, Robert denied it but behaved like someone who has been married to someone and doesn't care for her or their kids.

Victoria started scrolling the Facebook app, where she found a message from one of her classmates in school named Allen. he was a shy, dark, tall, fat guy from South Andhra Pradesh, who was her bench partner in class 6 in school. She remembered his face somehow, she started chatting with him online. He was very caring and responsible. They started to talk almost every day, as he was all alone not married at the age of 35, he had no one to talk to, slowly talking to each other for a year they became friends. He was a hardworking and responsible man for his family. Victoria actually wanted to meet Allen as he lived in Dehradun for some time for his work, she thought. She might gather some information about Robert as he often visited Dehradun and this place was close his hometown Muzaffarnagar. They decided to meet up. They met in a restaurant.

Eventually, they spoke about the school old days and so on. Then, Victoria picked up the topic of Robert's where she disclosed to him for the very first time that, she doubted that Robert is married to someone else as well. She requested him to find out information about Robert through his contacts in Dehradun. He agreed to help her out by seeking information from friends over there. He promised to deliver at least some information about Robert. They both departed to their respective homes. Victoria was thinking what if Robert comes to know that she met her guy friend Allen in his absence because she knew his mentality, then she thought when she is not wrong, why should shefear.

Allen contacted some of his colleagues in Dehradun, but as he asked them about this family, friends questioned him back "Why do you want to know about a criminal family?" People used to be afraid of Robert's father's Mr Samuel's name as he was Don of that state. So they refused to share any information and hung up the call, saying "its not their cup of tea".

Approaching a few people Allen came to the conclusion that this family was very famous in that area. His friends blocked him for asking for information about Don's son. Victoria was sinking day by day knowing that it was impossible to find out the truth about Robert's marriage. Days went by Victoria's health was falling down. Smoking increased for her.

At that time, she was in acute depression, she came to a conclusion when suicidal thoughts came to her continuously. Once when Darbie and her son were sleeping at night, she went to the terrace of the building and tried to jump down and commit suicide. She had nothing left with her, whatever she tackled since being a child till now. She was 35 years old now and nothing had changed, all the sufferings and guilt were there in her head and heart forever.

She tried to jump from the terrace with one leg out and then looked down, both her kid's faces appeared in front of her. She realized she has to be alive for her kids. She can't quit like this, she can't give up after coming so far. She came back home and kissed her kids. She decided to begin new only for her kids this time. She had sacrificed her entire life living for her father, mother, sister, and husband and now this was the time to live for kids, then she started reading books prescribed by sister Princess, "Who will cry when you die?". This book changed her complete perspective for Victoria towards life. There was no one to take care of her kids once she was gone. She had to survive for her kids.

Allen was talking to Victoria on daily basis, whereas Robert spoke to her once a week to take updates on the family. Victoria decided to meet Allen again but now along with her kids. They met in a mall watched a movie, and ate in a restaurant. Darbie didn't like Allen at first sight, as he was dark in colour, but after speaking to him, she realized he is a good person. Victoria never allowed her kids to be in touch with any of the male friends, or relatives in her family. The worst experience of childhood had an impact on her, she can't trust anyone anymore in regard to her kids.

Allen gifted a pen and wallet and chocolates to Victoria's kids. They spent a good time together even when Allen was a stranger to kids. They went home happy. After a week, Robert visited

Victoria and the kids after a long time. Victoria and the kids were happy to see him. They welcomed Robert with cake cutting and good food. Kids were grown-up now, Darbie was 14years old and Derrick was 9 years old. Watching other kids' dads, they also wanted to spend time with their dad. Robert's behaviour was changed in a good way.

Robert came to know that Victoria had accepted one friend request on Facebook sent from his cousin's sister's friend. He was annoyed to know that without asking him how she could accept some unknown friend request, he was so angry that he smashed her face with his wrist. Victoria directly got a hole on her upper lips because of the finger ring he was wearing. Blood started flowing like water from her lips, but Victoria did not react to it much as she was used to beating harder than this. She appeared to be composed but crying. Robert immediately went on his knees and apologized and asked her,"Is there a hole on your upper lips?" Victoria grabbed a cigarette and started smoking, and said, "Yes, even the smoke air is passing through the hole," in a sarcastic way. She had become a rock, a stone that could not feel physical pain. The next day she treated that wound with the doctor's help.

Victoria realized that Robert wouldn't change in his lifetime, he will be the same angry violent man throughout his life, just like her abusive alcoholic father. A few days passed by Robert returned back to the village.

Victoria was alone with her two kids. Allen became her friend, day by day they used to share every small detail of their daily activities with each other. Darbie always wanted to buy a pet dog Rottweiler whenever she watched others with pets since her childhood. Victoria was afraid of dogs, she never touched a dog before, when they had newly moved to Mumbai. Darbie had found a little dog puppy sleeping in a shoe outside a cake shop, shivering due to the cold as it was raining. She picked that puppy up and asked Victoria to take that puppy home, but Victoria thought that dog is not well and took it to the doctor vet where they treated the puppy and gave some medicines. The puppy was only 3 days old. They took the puppy home along with them and fed him milk and medicine within a few days puppy was well. They kept him for six months but couldn't take care of him anymore, they sent him lifetime boarding to one NGO that worked for dogs.

Now as Darbie was studying in grade 9, and COVID storm had already hit India. Schools were closed down. Darbie nagged Victoria to buy a puppy so that she can take care of him and be friends with him this year, next year she wouldn't get time, as it was her 10th board exam and she would be busy with her studies. Victoria discussed buying a puppy with Robert but he refused. Then one day while talking to Allen regarding it, he said it is a good idea to get kids engaged and get them good company in the form of pets. Darbie finally convinced Victoria to buy one small puppy, she searched and found one pet shop. From where they purchased a small puppy of 35 days Rottweiler, they named him Sky. He was a male dog. Victoria was so scared of dogs that she didn't even touch him earlier but gradually her fear of dogs disappeared and she started loving him. They bought a new family member for their home.

AUTHORS BIO DETAIL

The author, Supriya, is a 39 years old woman. She is a single mother of two children and one dog. She is practising "life coaching" for the past 2 years.

Supriya is the rarest type of woman who knows how to love with her whole heart. She would rather be alone than be with the wrong kind of people. She is not a sweet talker and people are often confused because she is so brutally honest, but you will never find the bigger heart in the universe. Whoever is loved by her is the luckiest person.

She fell, she crashed, she broke, she cried, she crawled, she hurt, she surrendered, and then she rose again.

She has healed herself more times than you can ever imagine. She wears her traumas like crowns.

She has wiped her tears before they had a chance to roll off her cheeks. She is a healer.

She is stronger because she had to be. She is smarter because of her mistakes, happier because of the sadness, and wiser because she learned

She knows the hurt of the world often lands on the broken, but the deeper the pain is, the stronger the wings are.

She is a strong woman who isn't just born that way; she was forged in the fires and strengthened through the storms.

Some days she is a warrior, some days she is a broken mess. Most days she is a bit of both. But every day she is there, standing, fighting, trying.

She believes that her fire is meant to be loved by the wild, not understood by the weak. The fire inside her will never be tamed by someone who doesn't have the courage to see the beauty in her chaos.

She says that she is not a victim for sharing her story, she is a survivor setting the world on fire with her truth and there might be someone in the world who needs her light, her warmth, and her raging courage.

She is an example of strength is what we get from the madness we survive.

She believes that you don't know how strong you are until you are pushed beyond what you thought you could handle and still emerge on the other side with more bravery, grace, and determination.